I dedicate this book to my loving wife, Molly,

who supported my adventures, most importantly, with her trust.

Foreword

When you first meet Jack, you may not realize he is an adventurer. First impressions tilt towards accountant or software engineer. Quiet and modest. Even though I have known Jack for almost 30 years, I had not heard half the stories contained in this memoir, "Above and Beyond". My first indication of his inner drive was noticed, oddly enough, on a basketball court. Playing pick-up basketball every day at the local high school, Jack, like me, was one of the older players, but he played baseline to baseline with impressive intensity and determination. Since then, Jack and I have collaborated on many Alaskan field studies and scientific publications.

I can see Jack pedaling a unique water-bike along 1,000 miles of Pacific coastline—into headwinds. I can see him piloting the first ever aerial waterfowl surveys across 2,000 miles of Siberian landscape. I can see him undertaking an extraordinary ocean kayak expedition. Throughout, I can imagine him tackling problems with his analytical mind and coming up with innovative solutions. If you were stuck in the Alaska Wilderness, you would want Jack Hodges by your side.

This book has two parts: the first describes his professional life, which was marked by many firsts— doing the kinds of things in boats and planes that will never be repeated in an era of governmental caution and safety regulations. Jack's survey plane, N754, which today hangs on display inside the Anchorage International Airport, is a symbol of that transition. This specially modified de Havilland Beaver with a turbine engine is one of a kind. Thus, it never received the expensive tests required by the Federal Aviation Administration to give it their stamp of "airworthiness". Yet it was flown dependably for decades, from Mexico to Siberia, without the slightest mishap. Now, the best wildlife survey aircraft in the world is a work of art, not a workhorse. A biologist and his plane, both retired.

The second part of the book is an enchanting story of the adventure and adversity that shapes a man. His love of wildlife and wild lands, his love of the people in his life— mentors, friends and family. His character, integrity, and philosophy shine throughout, and make this much more than a self-reporting memoir. It is the best kind of adventure story. A true story that we can enjoy from the comfort of our armchairs, knowing that there are people out there who go beyond, push the envelope, and live the kind of rich Alaska life many of us only dream about.

Mathew Kirchhoff (*Wildlife Biologist*)

Anchorage, Alaska - November 2017

Acknowledgements

Bruce Conant facilitated my career from start to finish. He quietly and persistently convinced Fred Robards to hire me after college, as the assistant bald eagle specialist. Bruce served as my airplane pilot on scores of bald eagle surveys, from Ketchikan to the Aleutian Islands. He showed me how an airplane could move beautifully in concert with the timbered shorelines, the steep fjords, and the myriad of islands. Ten years later, he hired me to be his assistant, as a waterfowl survey pilot and biologist. He gave me my earliest lessons about weather, the primary contributing factor to aircraft fatalities in Alaska. He showed me how to be patient when I was on the ground wishing I was in the air, and how to be smart when I was in the air wishing I was on the ground. He secured the best wildlife survey aircraft in the world for the waterfowl project and maintained that aircraft in near perfect condition. I was the benefactor of all of this. Jim King also seemed to recognize potential in me. He invited me to help with banding projects of geese in the interior of Alaska and on the north slope of Alaska. As with Bruce, Jim flew many surveys for me, and was another excellent aviation mentor. Phil Schempf, my supervisor while working with eagles, gave me a long leash and trusted me. Mike Jacobson, like Bruce, was a close friend and great companion for field work throughout my career. Andy Anderson was a top notch boat skipper for the bald eagle work. I took every opportunity to get out of my office and help Andy take care of the vessel, *SURFBIRD*. He taught me what I would need to know for when I became skipper of my own boat. Deb Groves sat next to me in the plane as we flew hundreds of hours of swan surveys and coastline waterbird surveys. She was the most diligent, dependable and competent aerial wildlife observer a person could hope for. Over the years, I had the invaluable and superbly professional support of three branch chiefs in Anchorage; Dirk Derksen, Russ Oates and Julian Fischer. They shouldered the bulk of the unpleasant governmental bureaucracy work – so that I could drive boats, fly airplanes and count birds. They trusted me and supported me, always. I am indebted to Heather Parker, Matt Kirchhoff, Dirk Derksen, Julian Fischer, Barbara Eldridge, Deb Groves and Bob Hutton for helping me with my manuscript. I owe much of my own character to my loving father, who gave me confidence in myself. However, I disappointed him when I flew to Russia in 1995 instead of participating in the Hodges family reunion that he had so masterfully orchestrated.

CONTENTS

Part One - Professional Life

Part Two - Personal Life

Appendices

Part One

Professional Life

Chapter 1 - First Flight into Siberia
1992

Siberia was beyond the curvature of the earth, somewhere in front of me. Alaska was out of sight behind me. I was suspended between the two great super powers. Russia expected me to enter their airspace at 1500 meters altitude, so I decided an altitude of 5000 feet was good enough. Over the Bering Sea, with almost 200 miles yet to go, I needed to trust my vintage float plane, N754. The gauges were reading normal, but the fuel pressure needle was vibrating. Was that normal? For some reason I wasn't sure. I told myself to trust my turbine engine. As long as it was getting fuel, it was supposed to be a superbly reliable engine. At this altitude, my radio could reach the American Flight Service Station in Nome for the majority of my 250 mile crossing. If I had to make an emergency landing, I would have plenty of time to relay my exact location and we would probably be rescued. The wheels on the floats were retracted, so we stood a good chance of remaining upright in the ocean. Now my ears started hearing a worrisome rhythmic surge in the engine. Am I imagining this too? I glanced over at my coworker and fellow biologist, Bill Eldridge. He appeared unconcerned. Everything must be okay. Just relax.

The Russian authorities had prohibited me from crossing into Siberia where Alaska kisses Russia. There, it would have been only a 50 mile crossing, with two tiny specks of land in the middle of that span, the Diomede Islands. Only 3.5 miles apart, the eastern one is ours and the western one is Russia's. When it is Friday on our side, it

1

is Saturday on their side. I wasn't allowed to cross at the Diomedes because that route would have taken me into proximity of a Russian radar installation.

Our plane, built in 1958, less than a decade into the Cold War, was now helping to eliminate that lengthy Russian – American standoff. Born in Canada, it began life as FAEC-29 in the Cuban Air Force. After Fidel Castro assumed power, it was shipped to the United States. In 1968 the U.S. Fish and Wildlife Service acquired it as a surplus aircraft from the U.S. military. The agency then transformed it into a world class wildlife survey aircraft, featuring a powerful Garrett turboprop engine. No other de Havilland beaver would ever look like it or preform like it. By 1972 it had already helped determine the boundaries of the 55 million acres of waterfowl habitat in Alaska that was to be added to the National Wildlife Refuge system.

This first flight to Russia was in July of 1992. As an Alaskan wildlife survey pilot and biologist for the U.S. Fish and Wildlife Service, I was tasked with piloting the Sberian mission. This would be the first time since World War II that a foreign plane attempted to fly unrestricted through the Russian military airspace of Siberia, at the nominal altitude of 100 feet in search of wildlife. Russian biologists knew what species of waterfowl were present in Siberia and roughly where they occurred, but they did not know the sizes of their bird populations. We in America were very concerned about several species that lived in both Alaska and Russia: the four species of eider ducks, as well as emperor geese and brant geese. In particular, the number of spectacled eider and Steller's eider had declined drastically in Alaska. If that was happening in Russia as well, our concern was doubled, and the ducks could be facing endangerment or even extinction. However, if, on the other hand, these birds were abundant in Russia, there would be less immediate concern about our North American populations.

As we drew closer and closer to Russia, the reality of the incredulous circumstance in which I found myself began to sink in. My mind drifted back 31 years to my earliest childhood memories about Russia. I was in fourth grade. My school was just six miles from Washington D.C. and the White House. The air raid alarm blared across the school's loud speakers every few months. All of my classmates and I squeezed under our wooden desks. Our teacher instructed us to protect the back of our heads with our hands. I was not scared. We did this often. We were told over and over what the real thing would be like. There would be an intensely bright light. We were told not to look at it, because it will burn your eyes. Then a huge blast of air will strike the school with terrible force, and all of the windows will spray glass. After the blast there will be radioactive dust settling onto everything.

This was my primary association with the Union of Soviet Socialist Republics (USSR) as a young child. For us, it seemed like the teachers must consider this a real possibility. Why else would we be practicing it? I thought, surely the Soviets would try to bomb the President. They had thousands of these bombs and they hated us so much that they just might get mad enough to launch them. We had plenty of bombs too, and our only hope was that they would be afraid to send bombs at us, because if they did, we would send our bombs back at them. Growing up, I thought the Soviet people hated us and they might attack at any time.

Now the relationship between Russia and the United States had changed dramatically. The date for our flight, July 27, 1992, had been established months before. I fretted about what kind of weather I would be facing for the crossing of the Bering Sea. As it turned out, luck was on our side. The weather was clear blue skies. It couldn't have been better.

Mountains began to take shape in front of us. As more and more definition was revealed, we could see that they were ominous and barren. I hadn't thought beforehand what to expect. Green hues were evident in the lower reaches of the mountains. The landscape reminded me of murals I had seen in museums showing woolly mammoths, and ice age people carrying spears in a treeless and harsh land. It was clear this land held deep intrigue.

First view of Siberia, Russia.

Provideniya was the small town where customs officials would accept or reject us. First I needed to land the plane. In the distance I saw the runway at the far end of a lake tucked between two mountains. It was gravel, and it slanted uphill away from us. It looked inviting. I was used to landing on gravel.

I touched down with considerable pride. As we taxied to the end of the runway I looked to the right of the terminal and noticed a tiny jet aircraft that seemed entirely out of place. Did they really land jets on this rough graveled runway? I tapped the right brake, turning us onto a sloped taxiway towards a modest blue and white wooden building. On the roof was a diminutive room with large windows all around, the control tower I presumed. A narrow platform and railing encircled it. A lone figure was standing at that railing, wearing a brown leather flight jacket. That must be Victor Shlyaev. Bill and I had met Victor a year earlier, in his hometown of Anadyr, 350 miles west of Provideniya. We had been in Anadyr to determine the feasibility of bringing an American aircraft to Russia. It was extremely good fortune that our paths had crossed with Victor's. What a wonderful sight to see our friend. He was a navigator with the Russian airline Aeroflot. He was now assigned to be our navigator for our flights in Russia. He would take care of us.

An official standing in front of our plane motioned to me where to park. Then two customs agents approached our plane on foot as Bill and I climbed out. With some broken English but mostly hand gestures, they asked us to remove our baggage. They began to poke through our survival gear, airplane supplies and life raft. I wasn't particularly alarmed until they asked if we had any hand-held radios. I said we had an emergency aircraft radio, and tried to emphasize how important it was to our safety if our primary VHF radio in the instrument panel failed, or we lost our electrical power. They said the portable radio was not allowed in Russia and they would hold it in their possession for the duration the plane stayed in Russia. I was reluctant to acquiesce because it seemed unnecessary for them to take it, but realized I had no power to argue. I was glad that they agreed to hold our life raft until we returned and departed their country for Alaska.

After clearing customs, we were immediately greeted by Victor. He came to us, extending his hand and shaking ours vigorously, flashing a big smile. We would later learn that his youthful face belied his experience, skill, toughness and iron resolve when dealing with other Russian officials. He was the perfect person to have with us for this undertaking. My crew was coming together nicely. Bill and I were a good team, both members of the Migratory Bird Management branch of the U.S. Fish and Wildlife Service in Alaska. Both of us were seasoned aerial observers. Bill brought a special talent for coping with challenges one often faces in foreign lands. He had worked in Chile, Mexico and various parts of Africa. He maintained a clear grasp of the overall picture. He figured out who the key players were and what potential problems we might be faced with. He was always developing a strategy to maximize our chances for success. I needed his skills, because I lacked them. I excelled more at focusing on and handling one problem at a time. I was analytically savvy. Bill was politically astute.

Our first order of business was to take on jet fuel. A large, unwieldy nozzle was extended to me as I knelt on the wing. I then had to carry it along the leading edge to the outboard filling point. When I squeezed the nozzle handle, fuel shot out under tremendous pressure. I could not make it flow slowly. I repeatedly released 5 second bursts of fuel into the wing tank, immediately shutting off the nozzle to prevent the fuel from spewing out of the tank. After each burst, I had to wait for the fuel to flow through baffles into the rest of the tank. Every time I shut off the fuel, the fueling crew on the ground screamed angry Russian chastisements at me. They were extremely upset, but I had to ignore them and get the fuel. I didn't have a clue what they were saying.

As it turned out, our U.S. currency didn't work in Provideniya. When it came time to pay for the fuel, the landing fee, the parking fee and the navigation aids fee, the airport official told us he could only accept rubles. We didn't have rubles. After much deliberation, Victor informed us that the solution was for the airport to find someone in town with enough rubles and a willingness to accept U.S. money for them. So about 45 minutes later the principal of the local high school drove up to the terminal on his motor scooter and we exchanged money. Only then did we have the ability to pay for our fuel and fees.

The next leg of our trip was to Victor's home airfield, Anadyr. We wanted to follow the coast at low level and scout for marine birds and get a feel for the land. Victor said he would ask for permission from the military, but he was skeptical. The Russian airspace was owned by the military. He showed us the regulation which pertained to foreign aircraft. The exact wording, in English was, "The whole of the U.S.S.R. territory, including its territorial waters, with the exception of airways, corridors in the state border, terminal and airport traffic zones, shall be deemed prohibited for being over flown by aircraft of foreign states."

An hour later we got our answer, "You do not have authorization for a foreign aircraft to fly such a route. You must fly the published airway at 1500 meters." We expected our luck to change once we got to Anadyr and had a chance to establish that we did indeed have authorization.

We put our personal gear back into the plane. Victor climbed into the right front seat. This was a great relief. He was a professional navigator, required on all *Aeroflot* flights. *Aeroflot* was the one and only airline in Russia. He was obviously competent. As soon as I had the engine running he began turning knobs on the instrument panel. It didn't bother me that he was touching my plane without asking. He was familiarizing himself with all of my radios. We had an HF radio, which we never used in America because no one monitored it anymore. It was the primary radio in Alaska from the 1940's through the 1960's, but was now outdated. Victor's eyes lit up when he saw it in the panel. This was still the most important radio in Russia. It could reach distant locations where the newer VHF radio would not reach, beyond mountains or past the curvature of the earth. Victor informed me that we would need this radio. All aircraft in Russia were required to make radio contact with the authorities once every 30 minutes. There was a 15 minute grace period, but if they had not heard from us within 45 minutes, a search would be immediately instigated. This was far more stringent than our system in America which could take many hours to begin a search. Victor then inspected the ADF, the VOR and the LORAN radios.

Victor, our navigator, friend and facilitator.

Victor handled the communications with the tower and we quickly left Provideniya behind. The mountains were dramatic and stark. The ocean was deep blue. A very long, narrow spit of land stretched ahead of us. The map showed that it was fully 40 miles in length. I wondered what marine bird species were there right now. Victor informed me that even if we had been given permission to fly at low level to Anadyr, we would not have been able to fly low over this long spit. It was fully protected as a walrus haul out area and aircraft were not allowed to fly below 1000 meters. I was surprised that the Russians had put into place regulations to protect a wildlife species.

Our landing at Anadyr was memorable. As we approached, I could see the runway was extremely long and wide. It was made of cement. Victor talked with the tower, in Russian, and interpreted the instructions to me. He pointed out that the west side of the runway was controlled by the military and the east side was controlled by *Aeroflot*. I looked at the military side and saw an amazing sight. Neatly lined up on the tarmac were at least two dozen Russian fighter jets. Their fighters were not housed in hangars like the American fighter jets in Alaska. Did they sit outside like this even in winter, I wondered to myself? These were the jets that would be scrambled if the Russians were under attack from America, or if an aircraft veered into Russian airspace. I was again glad to have Victor next to me. Victor looked at me and said, "Captain Jack, we should be higher in this part of the landing pattern. Do you see those small bunkers below us? Those are anti-aircraft missile positions." "Okay Victor, I will fly higher."

Landing was easy on this huge runway, but on the roll out after touch down, an unforeseen problem became evident. The cement runway was made of concrete tiles, or pads, each about 20 feet square. Frost and freezing had apparently lifted and tilted these pads so that our tires were whacking against the edges of the pads, like rolling into 3 inch high cement curbs every 20 feet. It rattled the airplane and rattled me to know that we would be subjecting the plane to this torture on every takeoff and landing. I turned the plane around on the runway and slowly back taxied to the *Aeroflot* area and was directed where to park.

A large crowd of people gathered around us. Their attention was focused mostly on the floats. They were trying to read the placards near the bow. It is probable that they had never seen an amphibious float plane. We were to see this response at nearly every airport.

Victor said that Bill and I would be staying with him at his apartment. We headed on foot to Victor's apartment to meet his wife, to celebrate, and to eat dinner. The apartment building was unlike anything I had ever seen. It was stark and uninviting to look at. It was made of cement. There was nothing but cement and gravel on the grounds outside the building. There wasn't a single plant in sight. We entered through a small door into a stairwell that reeked of a putrid stench. We climbed several flights of stairs, entered a gloomy hallway and then through another door into Victor's apartment.

The contrast of the apartment to what we had just seen of the building was disorienting. Whereas there was no pride in the building, there was obviously much pride in this apartment. Large, beautiful rugs hung on the walls. It was clean and very tidy. We met Lyuda. She was attractive, gracious, and a little bit bashful. She did not speak English, or was reluctant to try her English with us. Leaning against their mom were two adorable young girls. The oldest was about ten years old, the young one about four. Victor's family was the pride of his life. We soon settled in and felt entirely comfortable.

Victor informed us that he was very fortunate that his family did not have to occupy this apartment with any other families. The apartment consisted of three rooms plus a tiny kitchen and a bathroom. Until recently, a second family had lived in one of the rooms and shared the kitchen and bathroom with the Shlyaev family. He said that often there were three families in an apartment like his. The families had to stagger their meals. I wondered how they managed to share the tiny little bathroom.

Soon there was a knock on the door and Dr. Evgeni Syroechkovsky burst into the room. Evgeni, a biologist from Moscow, was in large part responsible for this improbable flight of an American airplane across the Russian landscape in search of birds. Evgeni did much prior work in Moscow arranging for the authorizations through the Minister of Defense. His political connections were at the highest levels of government and the military. I don't know how he acquired those connections, but they were necessary to pull this off. He was very excited to see us. He had travelled across 8 time zones to get to the Russian Far East. I judged him to be about 50 years old, short in stature but obviously strong in character and physique. Two years earlier, in 1990, the U.S. Fish and Wildlife Service had tried to get an American aircraft to this region. Evgeni had been instrumental in obtaining necessary permissions from the military for the low-level waterfowl surveys with that United States aircraft. This was prior to my involvement. He had even sent two of his biologists to a remote sand spit on the arctic coast to await the U.S. plane. That plane never came. At the last minute the Minister of Defense said "Nyet". Now when Evgeni saw our plane parked on the ramp, in his Russian homeland, he was full of joy. This was success. We thanked him for his efforts and told him how glad we were to finally see him face to face.

Evgeni was quite concerned when he heard that we had been denied permission to fly at low level today from Providentia to Anadyr, because he had procured all of the necessary authorizations. When he looked in his belongings for the paper with the military authorization number, he found he had left it in Moscow. He immediately left Victor's apartment to straighten things out and to arrange for overnight security for our plane, N754.

Later in the evening, he returned with the authorization number. His niece in Moscow was able to get it for him. We still did not know whether this number would work for us. Tomorrow we would learn more.

I had my own apprehensions. What challenges would I have to face with weather in this strange land? What would the other runways be like? Would our plane be safe from thievery? Would we do something wrong and end up in the middle of an international incident, or worse? My boss, Bruce Conant, was very nervous about my taking this special, one of a kind, wildlife survey aircraft to Russia. What if the authorities confiscated our plane? What if we had a major mechanical malfunction? We had taken the precaution of having two mechanics in Anchorage get official government passports and visas, in case we had to bring them to Russia on short notice.

I put my concerns aside. Bill and I brought out some smoked salmon to share with our hosts, knowing that food was difficult to obtain in eastern Siberia. Before we

8

even started to eat the salmon, Victor disappeared to the kitchen and returned with a can of meat which he opened to share with us. We were to learn that it was almost impossible to give things to the Russian people, because they would invariably give more to you in return. We were to see this over and over. It was either a code of honor or a matter of intense pride. It was an example of those with the least, giving the most.

Victor called the local officials to find out if our flight plan for the next day had been approved. We should have heard something by now. They in turn contacted their superiors in Khabarovsk. Victor was told that if our flight request was approved, it would be the first time a foreign plane had been allowed to fly off of published routes in Siberia since World War II. Evgeni had already obtained permission from a high level in the military, so we wondered what the problem was at this point. Evgeni called his friend in Moscow and had him call the Minister of Defense. We could only wait now. Evgeni told us that no word was better than a negative response. It indicated that they must be thinking about it.

Lyuda and her daughters, Victor's beautiful family in front of their apartment building.

The evening wore on and still no word. Victor told us that ordinarily by 9:00 pm there is word from Khabarovsk that all flight plans for the next day in the region of Anadyr are approved. This night, no flights in the region, *for any aircraft,* had been approved. Victor said this was highly unusual. Clearly we were creating a problem for air travel in this region.

Bill and I slept in Victor's daughter's room. The next morning we were the last to get up. When we saw Victor, he told us how his four year old daughter had wanted to go into her room. Victor explained to her that she couldn't do that because people were still sleeping in there. She looked up at him and said, "But daddy, those are not people. They cannot talk."

At 8:30am, Victor learned that all flight plans for Anadyr had been approved, *except for ours.* He left the apartment to meet Evgeni at his office. At 9:30am he returned to the apartment with a big smile on his face. This would be our day. The military had given us permission to fly low level flight paths to count birds, flying just 100 feet above the ground. Evgeni had somehow pulled it off. We didn't ask whom he knew or whom he had talked to. We were just glad he was there to make it happen. It was another beautiful sunny day and we were in a hurry to take advantage of it.

We quickly gathered our personal gear. It was important to get into the air before anything could change. We felt that once we had a flight under our belts, future flights would fall into place. As we walked toward the plane on the tarmac, we were starting to get giddy. Victor gave us a stern warning, "Do not behave as if you are happy. Only after we return, can we take a picture." So we pretended to be very serious, professional, and unemotional. In Alaska, I never wore my U.S. Fish and Wildlife Service uniform. I thought it was a bit silly for a biologist to wear one. But here, as an American pilot, I wanted to display my uniform and show that I was an official, just like any other pilot on this airfield.

We took off and headed for Egvekinot, a small mining town on the north shore of Kresta Bay. Victor was seated next to me in the copilot seat. Ordinarily Bill would have sat there as the observer on the right side. Because Victor required access to all of the radios, Bill had to sit in the rear seat and make his observations from there. Evgeni was behind me in the other rear seat. We landed and topped off our fuel tanks before going on to the arctic coast. An important goal of ours was to fly the arctic coast to Cape Schmidt, but our original request for permission to fly in the Anadyr region had been interpreted by the Russians to mean the region administered by the Anadyr offices. Since Cape Schmidt was administered from Pevek, a different regional office, we were not allowed to fly to, or to land at, Cape Schmidt.

When we arrived at Kolyuchin Bay, we ran into extensive fog, which only allowed us to survey a portion of its shore. Meanwhile our destination airport, Lavrentiya, went from clear skies to heavy fog. We had sufficient fuel to overfly Lavrentiya to Provideniya for fuel, which we did. Then we headed back to Anadyr, having spent 6.7 hours in the air and covering a very large area. We parked the plane and climbed out. Now was the time for smiles, and pictures were taken to document this historic occasion. How very far I had come since huddling under my desk in grade school. How very far our two countries had come towards sanity. It was a great feeling to be a small part of that transition.

Smiling after completing our ground breaking flight in Siberia, 1992.
Evgeni, the author, Victor and Bill.

We were seeing tremendous interest in our plane. Victor told me, "There is a line of 20 pilots that want to get a ride in N754". It was indeed a special airplane. When it lifted off of the runway we immediately entered a steep angle of climb that was bound to capture the attention of anyone watching. We were required to keep the air speed at 80mph (70 knots) after takeoff to reduce stress on the front landing gear while it was being retracted. Since the engine was at a high power setting, a steep climb was mandatory. Add a turn, and it appeared to outside observers that we were executing an aerobatic chandelle. Indeed, one time in Alaska, a citizen reported to the FAA that they had seen N754 doing an aerobatic maneuver after takeoff. Our chief flight instructor straightened it out with FAA, saying those flight maneuvers were standard operating procedure for N754. The plane was unique in other ways, too. Besides its excellent climb performance, it had visibility from the cockpit comparable to a helicopter. It carried 262 gallons of fuel which translated to 7 hours of flight time at our survey speed of 96 miles per hour. The propeller thrust could be placed in reverse for taxiing backwards on the water.

The following day, we had to wait until 10:30am for the fog to lift. We didn't get much work accomplished before we had to return to Anadyr. The wind had increased to 30 knots, and it was a direct crosswind to the runway. The operator's manual for N754 stated that the maximum crosswind component advised for safe landing on

11

these floats was 15 knots. I knew it would be very challenging to attempt it with 30 knots. I looked around for a lake as an alternative, but the ponds were too small. Towards the far end of the runway was a taxiway perpendicular to the runway. The runway was wide, at least 200 feet. The taxiway was at least 300 feet long, which would give me a total distance of at least 500 feet and straight in line with the wind. That is what I wanted. Because I would be landing into the strong wind, I would have a very short roll out. I said to Victor, "Tell the tower I want to land on one of the short taxiways into the wind." He keyed the mic and I could hear the conversation with the tower, in Russian.

Victor told me they had denied my request and that we were to land on the runway. I thought for a moment. Then I decided to demonstrate to the tower what landing on the runway meant for this airplane. I continued on the approach. I lined up with the runway and brought N754 down as if to land. I knew I wouldn't actually land the plane. In order to stay on the centerline of the runway, I had to hold a very large crab angle. That meant the plane was not facing down the runway, but rather was facing 45 degrees to the left. From inside the plane it felt as if we were flying sideways. From the tower I hoped it would look like an accident waiting to happen.

Just before touching down, I added full power and climbed up to pattern altitude, feeling more relaxed as the long runway grew smaller below me. I turned to Victor and told him to ask them again if I could land on the taxiway. He spoke to them again. His tone of voice took on a more urgent nature. There was considerable exchange between Victor and the tower, and then a long pause. The tower finally responded. Victor relayed to me. "You may land on the taxiway, but the pilot must take full responsibility for the landing." I smiled, and told Victor to tell them that I would take full responsibility. That's the way I viewed all of my landings, my sole responsibility. I was taught that I should do whatever it takes to land the plane in the safest possible way. If it requires declaring an emergency, then do so. Dealing with officials can take place while you are on the ground - afterwards. The great majority of the time, the officials will not cause much hassle because of your caution.

I started putting my full attention onto the task. I picked a taxiway near the far end of the runway. I lined up with it and set up for my landing. My intent was to use a short field landing technique of slow airspeed, lots of power, and touch down right at the edge of the taxiway to give myself maximum room for rollout. Our approach speed was quite slow due to the headwind, I saw that a military fuel truck had driven into view and stopped crossways, right on the taxiway where I was planning to touch down. Although the military had not been in communication with Victor, they must have been listening to his conversation with the civilian tower and disapproved. I was determined to get my plane on the ground safely, and this truck was trying to stop me from doing that.

Bill said, "What are you going to do Captain Jack?" I replied, "I am going to call their bluff." I decided I would just keep coming in, and basically play chicken with the driver of the military truck. I wasn't going to try to land over the top of him and greatly reduce the landing distance available to me. I headed straight for the truck, as if I didn't even know it was there. Just seconds away from reaching the truck, the driver moved the truck forward, out of my way. I flared and touched down at my planned spot, put the propeller into reverse, retracted the flaps and braked hard. The plane stopped on the taxiway before even reaching the runway. I had used only one third of the distance available to me.

When we stopped, Victor turned to me, "Captain Jack. Very good landing . . . but next time, please could you touch down maybe 20 meters further beyond the edge of the pavement?" I smiled, but didn't agree to accommodate him. Later, I had time to think about that military truck and ponder why they drove in front of me. That side of the runway belonged to the military and I think they were trying to assert their authority and keep me out of their area. I suspect the driver decided it would be better to move out of my way than to cause this funny looking airplane to crash.

The taxiway used to land sideways to the runway at Anadyr.

After we had parked, I told Victor he didn't need to call me Captain. He smiled and said that in Russia there are two rules when flying. "Rule one: The Captain is always right. Rule two: If the Captain is wrong, see rule one." I liked those rules. After that, the name "Captain Jack" stuck and became a term of endearment for Victor, and also for Bill.

The day after my taxiway landing, August 1, was a Saturday. We wondered if our taxiway landing on the military side of the runway yesterday had caused a big stir, because permission for our flight plan was denied. We might be out of business until Tuesday, after contacts were made in Moscow on Monday. We accepted an invitation from the head of airport security to go for a ride in his jeep. He took us to the river bank where we saw some people fishing with nets extended out into the water on long poles. We stopped to talk with one of them and he gave us a chum salmon.

When we got back to Victor's apartment, to our great surprise, Evgeni said word had been received giving permission for our flight. We hurried with preparations and took off at 1:30pm. For the next 3 hours we worked our way up the Anadyr River to Markovo. The river was beautiful, clear and wide. It meandered through colorful marshlands, groves of trees, and sometimes tundra. The wetland complex near Markovo was exceptionally rich and lush. Moose were abundant, as were whooper swans. Grizzly bears were seen on several occasions. The Russians told us that just 15 years ago there were several hundred thousand bean geese in the area. Now only a few small flocks totaling about 600 geese were evident on our flight path. We learned that the Russians blamed this decline on market hunting on the wintering grounds in China. Some of this wetland area we flew over had been designated as a swan reserve. We saw 45 swans with 6 broods.

The following day I was hoping to take some of the top *Aeroflot* officials for a ride in N754. Most of them were busy with something else because it was Sunday. We were at least able to take the chief of the control tower for a flight. He was the person that took responsibility for our landing on the taxiway. He was very appreciative of the opportunity to fly in our special plane.

Our trip to eastern Siberia was a success. We had firmly demonstrated that an American aircraft could operate smoothly in the new, post-Cold War Russian political environment. The outlook for future endeavors of this kind was very promising. It was fairly expensive to conduct these surveys. Besides fuel costs, we were charged $0.30 per kilometer flown ($0.50 per mile), $36 per landing, $4 per day for parking, and $4 per day for overnight security. The navigator fee was $65 per day plus $180 for each day we were airborne.

Our surveys did not cover the region comprehensively, especially the inland areas. However, we counted 10,000 eiders, 8,000 brant, over 5,000 emperor geese and 5,000 white-fronted geese. Sandhill cranes were abundant in the upland areas. Ducks were not particularly abundant but included northern pintail, scaup, scoters, wigeon, green-winged teal and mergansers. These were all species that Alaska shares with eastern Siberia. We also counted virtually all mammals that we could see, including bears, caribou, reindeer, foxes and wolves. There had been no comparable aerial survey of any of these species prior to our effort.

Victor accompanied Bill and me back to Provideniya, our departure point for the flight home. We said good-bye, telling Victor that we would do our best to return next year and continue the momentum which had been started. He said he would do his best to make sure he was our navigator again. We could not have found a better navigator and companion. He was delightful, superbly competent, loyal, and a great negotiator with the Russian authorities. I truly hoped we would see him again.

Bering Air was a small airline that operated out of Nome in 1992. They provided flights to Provideniya from Alaska with their small twin engine airplane. As we were taxiing to leave Provideniya for Nome, the *Bering Air* flight was also preparing to depart. Both of our planes were required to file a flight plan and both would be assigned the same altitude, 1500 meters (about 5000 feet). I was leaving shortly before the *Bering Air* plane. There was a low and solid cloud ceiling at about 1200 feet. The Russians required and expected me to climb into the clouds up to 5000 feet, but I wasn't going to comply. I was prohibited by my own agency from flying on instruments. Our method of flying in Alaska was to always keep visual contact with the ground. As I was taxiing for takeoff, the pilot of the *Bering Air* plane called me and asked me to put one of my radios on frequency 123.45. I told him "Roger". After takeoff, I throttled back to stay below the 1200 foot ceiling, as Provideniya faded behind me. *Bering Air* was cleared for takeoff a few minutes later headed in the same direction. Soon I heard the *Bering Air* pilot on 123.45 say "N754 this is Bering 6192R."

I responded, "This is N754, go ahead."

He came back with, "N754, what altitude are you REALLY going to fly at?"

"I will be at 1000 feet."

"Roger, I figured you would be staying low."

The Bering Sea below didn't seem as hostile heading this direction, towards Nome, towards home. The airports would be familiar, the Flight Service attendants would speak my own language, and any mechanical problems could be solved by our mechanics and our parts department. Nonetheless, I had felt surprisingly comfortable flying in Siberia. We had been shown much respect for our knowledge, abilities and aircraft. We had truly made contact.

This was the first of six missions that would take us deep into Siberia and almost half way to Moscow. Many more adventures lay ahead, and we would become the first foreign plane to land at several airports. But my career began in Alaska with bald eagles and boats, not waterfowl and airplanes.

My favorite eagle photo, 1977 with a Leica SLR and 200mm lens.